From
the
Library of

*I*n these pages I find solace.
This is my place, my time, my thoughts.
Let me see the world as
Anne Shirley did when she said,
". . . isn't it nice to think that
tomorrow is a new day with
no mistakes in it yet?"
I imagine myself at Green Gables
where anything is possible and
hope soars freely. With each
new day I'll raise my chin,
count my blessings, and
reach for the stars.

DONNA GREEN
Prince Edward Island
July, 1996

Oh, Miss Cuthbert, did you really say that perhaps you would let me stay at Green Gables? . . . Did you really say it? Or did I only imagine that you did?

*It's a serious thing to grow up, isn't it? . . .
it's a great responsibility because I have
only the one chance.*

I suppose you are used to sleeping in spare rooms. But just imagine what you would feel like if you were a little orphan girl who had never had such an honor.

What a splendid day! . . . I pity people who aren't born yet for missing it. They may have good days, of course, but they can never have this one.

Gracious heavenly Father. . . . Please let me stay at Green Gables; and please let me be good-looking when I grow up.

I'm going to imagine that I'm the wind that is blowing up there in those tree tops. When I get tired of the trees I'll imagine I'm gently waving down here in the ferns.

Oh, but it's good to be alive and to be going home . . . I've had a splendid time—it marks an epoch in my life. But the best of it all was the coming home.

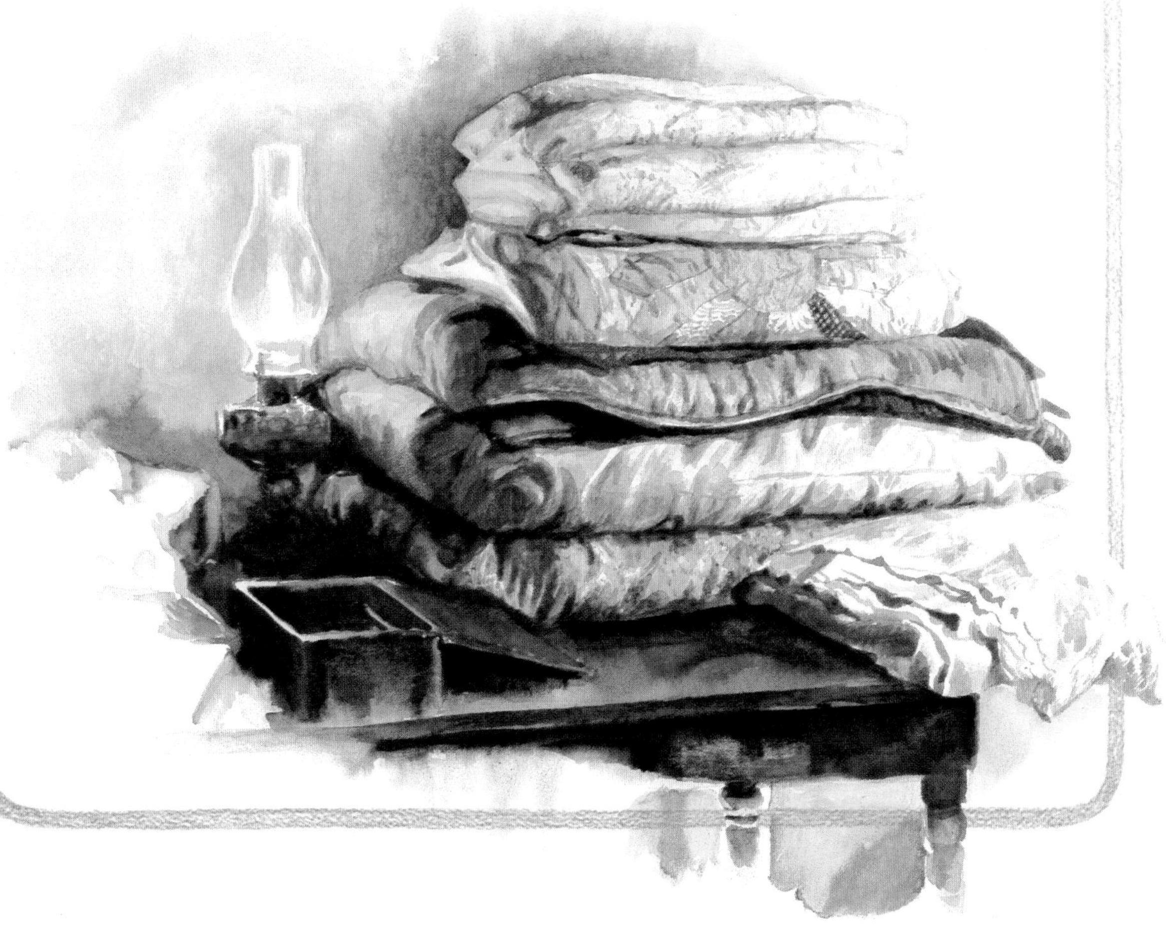

There must be a limit to the mistakes one person can make, and when I get to the end of them, then I'll be through with them. That's a very comforting thought.

No matter how hard I try to be good I
can never make such a success of
it. . . . But don't you think the trying so
hard ought to count for something?

This Island is the bloomiest place. I just love it already, and I'm so glad I'm going to live here.

Five minutes ago I was so miserable I was wishing I'd never been born and now I wouldn't change places with an angel!

I'm so glad I live in a world where there are Octobers. It would be terrible if we just skipped from September to November, wouldn't it?

*It's nicer to think dear, pretty thoughts
and keep them in one's heart, like treasures.*

Don't you feel as if you just loved the world on a morning like this?

There should have been a special commandment against nagging.

Listen to the trees talking in their sleep. . . .
What nice dreams they must have!

Don't be very frightened. . . . I expect I have sprained my ankle—I might have broken my neck. Let us look on the bright side of things.

*It gives you a lovely, comfortable feeling
to apologize and be forgiven, doesn't it?*

I'm so glad it's a sunshiny morning. But I like rainy mornings real well, too. You don't know what's going to happen through the day, and there's so much scope for imagination.

We're studying agriculture now and I've found out at last what makes the roads red. It's a great comfort.

*M*rs. Barry had the very best china set out. Nobody ever used their very best china on my account before.

You see before you a perfectly happy person . . . in spri

my red hair. Just at present I have a soul above red hair.

I love Miss Stacy with my whole heart. . . . When she pronounces my name I feel _instinctively_ that she's spelling it with an _e._

It's such a solemn thing to be almost fourteen. . . . It's perfectly appalling to think of being twenty. It sounds so fearfully old and grown up.

If I wasn't a human girl I think I'd like to be a bee and live among the flowers.

I imagine a good deal, and that helps to pass the time.

That's one good thing about me. I never do the same naughty thing twice.

I make so many mistakes. But then just think of all the mistakes I don't make.

It would be so much easier to imagine I was the Lady Cordelia if I had a real amethyst brooch on.

*Isn't it nice to think that tomorrow is a
new day with no mistakes in it yet?*

Dear old world . . . you are very lovely, and I am glad to be alive in you.

Isn't the breath of the mint delicious? . . .

$\mathcal{I}$'m tired of being studious and ambitious. I mean to spend at least two hours tomorrow lying out in the orchard grass, thinking of absolutely nothing.

Mustn't it be splendid to be remarkable and have compositions written about you after you're dead? Oh, I would dearly love to be remarkable.

Matthew always liked those roses the best. . . .
I hope he has roses like them in heaven.

There are some people . . . that you can love right off . . . . and there are others . . . that you have to try very hard to love.

Kindred spirits are not so scarce as I used to think. It's splendid to find out there are so many of them in the world.

Isn't it splendid to think of all the things there are to find out about?

It just makes me feel glad to be alive—it's such an interesting world.

Dear me, there is nothing but meetings and partings in the world.

I solemnly swear to be faithful to my bosom friend, Diana Barry, as long as the sun and moon shall endure.

Look at that sea—all silver and shadow and vision of things not seen.

The world looks like something God had just imagined for His own pleasure, doesn't it?

Next to trying and winning, the best thing is trying and failing.

I'm thirteen years old today. . . . *W*hen
I woke this morning it seemed to me that
everything must be different.

Oh, it's delightful to have ambitions. Just as soon as you attain to one ambition you see another one glittering higher up still.

I believe I could be a model child if I were just invited out to tea every day.

That is the first time I was ever called 'Miss.'
Such a thrill as it gave me! I shall cherish
it forever among my choicest treasures.

It's been my experience that you can nearly always enjoy things if you make up your mind firmly that you will.

And you know one can dream so much
better in a room where there are pretty things.

One can't stay sad very long in such an interesting world, can one?

I'm so glad my window looks east into the sunrising. . . . It's new every morning, and I feel as if I washed my very soul in that bath of earliest sunshine.

It's lovely to be going home and know it's home. . . . I love Green Gables already, and I never loved any place before. No place ever seemed like home.

It's always been one of my dreams to live near a brook. I never expected I would though. Dreams don't often come true, do they?

The illustrations in this book were painted by Donna Green in watercolor with colored pencil on Canson Aquarelle acid free watercolor paper. ◆ The artist also hand lettered the title of the book and decorative initials for each excerpt from *Anne of Green Gables* by adapting from Le Griffe which was first set by Solotype Typographers, Inc., Oakland, CA. ◆ The text for the journal pages was set in 24 point Nuptial Script and the front and back matter text was set in Fournier by Trufont Typographers, Inc., Hicksville, NY. ◆ Photography was the work of Gamma One Conversions, New York, NY. ◆ Color separations were made by Cromolit, S.A., Esplugues de Llobregat, Barcelona. ◆ Excerpts from speeches by Anne were selected and arranged by Victoria Fremont. ◆ Book and cover design created by Carol Belanger Grafton. ◆ Danielle French, Jessica Green, and Lindsay Hayden served as models for the characters of Anne and Diana. ◆ Invaluable assistance was provided by the staff and guides at Green Gables, P.E.I. ◆ This book was printed on 170gsm recycled matte art paper and bound in Spain by Book Print, S.L., Barcelona.